CREATURE PEOPLE

VOLUME ONE of THREE

Lon Chaney
Jack Pierce
The Westmores
Hammer Films
Dick Smith
John Chambers
Rick Baker
Stan Winston
Ve Neill
Greg Cannom
Kevin Yagher
Steve Johnson
Rob Bottin
Michael Westmore
Michele Burke
Phil Tippett
Tom Burman
Todd Tucker
Chris Walas

Written and Published by Scott Essman
Layout by Hauntorama
Photos Used Strictly for Publicity Purposes

Select Photos by the Creature People Themselves
Other Photos Courtesy of Various Contributors

Special Thanks to Sterling Long-Colbo
Extra Special Thanks to Bob Burns

© Copyright 2008, Scott Essman and VISIONARY MEDIA.
Correpondence: visionarycinema@yahoo.com
P.O. Box 1722, Glendora, CA 91740
(626) 963-0635

SCOTT ESSMAN

Lon Chaney: Man of 1000 Makeups

Though artists including John Chambers, Dick Smith, and Rick Baker brought inventive character makeups to a new level, the craft known as "special makeup effects," goes back to the inception of cinema. Silent film actors were often required to design and apply their own makeups when playing bit parts of Indians, old men, and historical figures. Significantly, three men started in the earliest years of film as actors who created their own characters with the use of personal makeup techniques. Jack Pierce and Jack Dawn started as actors and eventually switched to makeup full time in the 1920s. Each of them went on to run studio makeup departments and create legendary characters. A third man stayed true to his acting roots while furthering his makeup talents in order to get jobs in Hollywood. His name was Lon Chaney.

Lon Chaney (above, sans makeup) was a master of disguise, as evidenced by his numerous film roles. Pictured right is Chaney in "London After Midnight," and below is Chaney as the memorable "Phantom of the Opera."

Among his numerous creations, Chaney made cinema history with his legendary "Hunchback of Notre Dame," and "Phantom of the Opera" characters. Essentially, Chaney brought to the moviegoing public how effectively makeup could transform an actor into a different character. Due to Chaney's skills, audiences realized that one actor could play an infinite amount of different roles. The Hunchback (1923) and the Phantom (1925) were so stirring not only because they were frightening and memorable in and of themselves, but also because Chaney had so drastically transformed his face in each role.

Chaney created another great horror character in 1927 with his vampire in "London After Midnight." The ghastly image of the vampire, in long hat and fangs, is one of the iconic horror images of the silent era. However, Chaney used his makeup and acting talents to create a host of non-horror characters at the time. With the secretive materials in his makeup case, Chaney could become a crippled character, a woman, an old man, a clown, or just about anything that a script called for.

With the advent of sound film in the late 1920s, there were dramatic increases in the need for and development of special makeup, leading to the introduction of "the makeup artist." At Universal Studios, Jack Pierce brought the most timeless of monsters to life, including Frankenstein, the Wolf Man, and the Mummy. In 1939, "The Wizard of Oz" presented Jack Dawn's iconic fantasy characters, a landmark in the use of prosthetics for the alteration of actors' faces. Ironically or not, Chaney died in 1930 just as Universal was casting "Dracula." Whether or not Chaney would have been lured back to his first studio to create the Count is unknown, but Chaney's work in the 1920s surely stands the test of time. His work and makeup methods are still vitally studied today.

SCOTT ESSMAN

Jack Pierce The Man Behind the Monsters

As we look back on the cinematic pioneers of the 20th century, no individual is more significant in his field than genius makeup artist Jack Pierce, the legendary monster-maker who worked in the 1930s and 1940s at Universal Studios during their classic horror period.

In 1930, "Dracula" was first produced, and though Béla Lugosi refused to let Pierce apply his makeup (the actor had come from the stage where he always did his own work), Pierce came up with the styling for the vampire character and his many female victims. Immediately following the success of "Dracula," Junior wanted a follow-up, which led to the production of

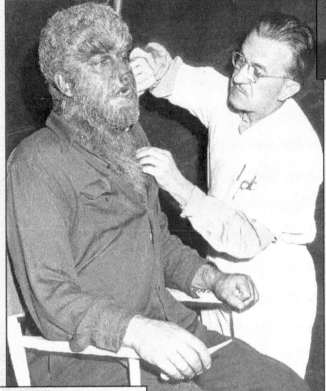

Jack Pierce (pictured above) applies hair to Lon Chaney, Jr., in "The Wolf Man." At top right is Pierce's "toned-down" make-up on Claude Rains' as the "Phantom of the Opera." At left, Boris Karloff as one of Pierce's most memorable creations.

"Frankenstein: in 1931. Though many have argued as to whether director James Whale, actor Boris Karloff, or Junior himself contributed to the makeup, the driving force behind the look of the character unquestionably belonged to Jack Pierce. Every morning, Karloff sat for four uncomfortable hours, suffering the makeup's high levels of toxicity, as Pierce and his assistants applied the head, facial buildup and layers of padding and costume modifications that would make him into the movies' most memorable monster. For the 43-year-old Karloff and 42-year-old Pierce, it was a remarkable achievement; their legend would have been guaranteed even if they had stopped their unique artist-performer collaboration right then and there.

Furthering their reputation, though, Pierce and Karloff teamed the following year to create "The Mummy." Though the actual creature is only seen on film for a matter of seconds, it was another unforgettable achievement in cinema horror when Im-Ho-Tep came alive and paraded across an unearthed Egyptian tomb. Karloff spent most of the picture as Ardath Bey, another Pierce incarnation, as the doomed prince looking for his lost bride.

Revamping his first version of the monster for "Bride of Frankenstein," Pierce also created the famous makeup and designed the electric hairstyle for Elsa Lanchester's bride. Once again, Pierce created an iconic movie character who only appeared on screen very briefly at the end of the film. For Béla Lugosi, with whom Pierce had locked horns several years earlier on "Dracula," Pierce created Ygor in 1939's "Son of Frankenstein." Conceived as a man who couldn't be hanged, the gnarled-toothed wretch became Lugosi's most original character in years.

Two years later, Pierce pulled out all the stops for "The Wolf Man" with Lon Chaney, Jr. in the title role. Though the two did not reportedly get along—Chaney did not like wearing the makeup or undergoing the lengthy application and removal period—Pierce excelled again with his werewolf concept, utilizing a design he had created for Karloff a decade earlier. Originally intended as a B movie, "The Wolf Man" was a true horror classic, and Pierce's version of the character has been the model for the numerous werewolves that have since come to the screen.

The final, original Pierce makeup arrived in 1943 with "Phantom of the Opera." Starring Claude Rains, it would be the only Jack Pierce monster movie shot in color. Though his treatment of Rains' makeup—revealed only at the end of the film—was cut down at the request of the producers (Pierce's original concept was considered too hideous!), it stands as another horror movie landmark.

In the 1940s, there were many monster sequels at Universal, many of which featured a version of The Mummy, The Monster, Count Dracula, or the Wolf Man, and Jack Pierce did the makeup on all of them. Lon Chaney, Jr. played all of the monsters at one time or another! The last Universal Frankenstein of the Jack Pierce era was Glenn Strange who played the monster twice for Pierce and once in "Abbott and Costello Meet Frankenstein."

Jack Pierce's reign at Universal ended shortly after WWII when the studio merged with International Pictures and replaced many of its department heads. He had been a makeup supervisor for 19 years and worked at the studio for 30 years, but Pierce ended his career working in low-budget independent films and television projects during the final 20 years of his life. Unthinkably, he died in virtual obscurity in 1968, but his work stands up today as landmark horror cinema.

Above: Pierce applies his classic "Mummy" make-up to Karloff for the memorable creature that appeared for just moments throughout the film. At right, Elsa Lanchester's electric hairdo from "The Bride of Frankenstein" is just another of Pierce's many definitive make-up creations.

SCOTT ESSMAN

The House of Westmore

In the history of the modern American movies, there are but few legacies of makeup artists. Only one family features four working generations: the Westmores of Hollywood. With ties to virtually every studio in the annals cinema, the Westmores created classic makeups back to the earliest years of silent film.

At the turn of the century, the patriarch of the English immigrants, George, was a wigmaker in his homeland. Later, he set up the first makeup department at any studio during the silent era. All of his six sons (he also had a daughter) became prominent makeup artists, running studio departments and making their names in makeup artistry through the century.

Starting at Paramount studios was Wally Westmore, responsible for creating one of the earliest onscreen "transformation" scenes for 1932's "Dr. Jekyll and Mr. Hyde," starring Frederic March. In the film, March creates a believably kind and gentle Dr. Jekyll until his consumption of a treacherous formula results in the animalistic Mr. Hyde.

When the character changes from doctor to demon and back, Westmore utilized several techniques with the special effects department. First, time-lapse photography was used where the camera would stop and March would get into Westmore's chair for one stage of transformation. March would be placed in the exact same position and the camera would start again, so that on film, he would appear to dissolve from one incarnation to the next. For certain moments, the actor would maintain the exact same position, and with the camera off, Westmore would attend to him right on the set! Still, for other seamless transitions, Westmore would use a reddish color to achieve the makeup, and with a red filter over the camera lens (the film was black and white and the red would never appear), it would hide the makeup until the desired moment. The red filter would be removed, revealing the hideous change into Mr. Hyde. After Westmore's work in this film, the concept of the transformation scene was appropriated by everyone from Jack Pierce to Jack Dawn in coming years.

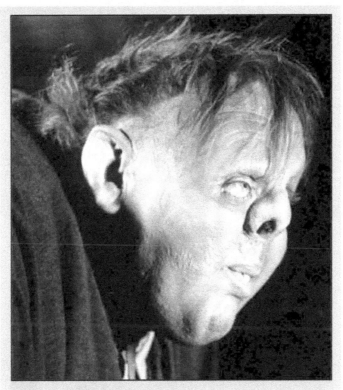

Perc Westmore's prosthetic makeup for Charles Laughton in "The Hunchback of Notre Dame" was a groundbreaking use of foam rubber in makeup design. Below, Bud Westmore had the task of replicating some of Jack Pierce's classic makeups for "Abbott and Costello Meet Frankenstein." His makeup was simpler, and lighter, much to the actors' delight.

Following the great success of "Dr. Jekyll" (March won an Academy Award for best actor), the following year, Westmore created the first screen version of H.G. Wells' "Island of Lost Souls," followed by numerous makeup achievements throughout Wally's career.

Perc Westmore was the department head at Warner Bros. where he worked on numerous classic films, including "Casablanca." In 1939 he was brought to RKO by their department head, Mel Berns to work on a big prosthetics project, a sound remake of "The Hunchback of Notre Dame." Though

Berns had an entire building and 33 hairdressers and makeup men under him at the department, his friend, Perc, had been brought in to create the prosthetic makeup pieces for star Charles Laughton.

At that same time, there had been key developments in the use of prosthetics on films including Jack Dawn's "The Good Earth." Then, with the assistance of the Bau brothers – George and Gordon – a new type of foam rubber was being developed. It made the concept of applying complicated makeups to actors' faces much easier for makeup artists and more comfortable for actors. Thus, Perc developed a complete makeup for Laughton, including a deformed face and gruesome hump, and the Baus were responsible for making the foam rubber – often called latex – which made up the materials for the hunchback makeup.

Seen most prominently in the horrifying whipping on the pillory, Laughton's makeup was a resounding success for both Westmore and the Bau brothers, who would go on to revolutionize prosthetics in films in the ensuing decades.

After Jack Pierce left Universal Studios in 1947, Bud Westmore ran their department for the next quarter century. Utilizing many of the techniques that his brother Perc and the Bau brothers initiated, Bud simplified Pierce's handmade makeup methods to the delight of his actors. Using prosthetic appliances to create character makeups, Westmore also shortened the makeup process.

One of his first major assignments was replicating Pierce's horror characters for the comic romp, "Abbott and Costello Meet Frankenstein." In place of Pierce's choice to build up the Frankenstein Monster's massive head by hand every day, Bud Westmore recruited veteran Jack Kevan to create Glenn Strange's Monster using a foam rubber head. Similarly, under Westmore's direction, Emile LaVigne, most notable for creating the Tin Man makeup in "The Wizard of Oz," created The Wolf Man for "Meet Frankenstein" using prefabricated foam rubber appliances. Additionally, Béla Lugosi, 17 years after he appeared in the original "Dracula," reprised his role as The Count. The horror-comedy was an unqualified hit and put Westmore on the same plane as his famous brothers.

Above: Bud Westmore's foam rubber suit for Ben Chapman and Ricou Browning in "Creature From the Black Lagoon" remains a classic chiller to this day. At right, Wally Westmore's transformation of Frederic March into Mr. Hyde helped March win an Academy Award.

In 1954, the Universal makeup department was tasked with the huge job of creating the title character in "Creature From the Black Lagoon." With Kevan, sculptor Chris Mueller, designer Millicent Patrick, and a young Bob Dawn – son of MGM's Jack Dawn – in the laboratory, Westmore's team devised a foam rubber suit for actor Ben Chapman and swimming double Ricou Browning. The classic monster reappeared in two 1950s sequels.

In subsequent years, Bud got many choice assignments, including the Lon Chaney biography, "Man of a Thousand Faces." Again, he and Kevan used foam rubber appliances to re-create many of Chaney's classic makeups, using actor James Cagney. Though Cagney's round face was in contrast to Chaney's long rectangular head, Westmore and Kevan suggested the original makeups, such as the Hunchback of Notre Dame, without replicating them.

By the early 1970s, five of the six Westmore brothers had passed away – brother Frank lived and wrote a definitive family biography, "The Westmores of Hollywood" – but their offspring continued the makeup legacy. Even today, the Westmore name is prominent in makeup artistry, with younger family members entering the business on a regular basis.

SCOTT ESSMAN

Hammer Films: Horror, British-Style

When the successful Universal horror cycle had run its course in the late 1950s, the studios ceased the production of monster movies and started making similarly-budgeted science-fiction films. In the 1950s, aside from Universal's "Creature from the Black Lagoon" series, no original monsters appeared in American cinema that stood on two legs. However, a British film company called Hammer began producing color versions of the classic monster stories. Though they needed to change their monster likenesses so as not to emulate the Universal monsters, Hammer endeavored to produce films featuring the characters of the Frankenstein Monster, Count Dracula, Phantom of the Opera, mummy, and werewolf.

To get the jobs done cheaply and memorably, Hammer brought in British makeup artists who had previously excelled in non-horror films. First up was Phil Leakey, who created an original Frankenstein Monster on actor Christopher Lee in 1957's "Curse of Frankenstein." Using a group of simple appliances and scars, Leakey made Lee's Monster a frightfully unforgettable character.

The next year, Lee played the Count in "Horror of Dracula" and in 1959, he played the lead in "The Mummy," both with basic makeups by Roy Ashton. However, it was Ashton's next assignments that were his classics. In 1961, with newcomer Oliver Reed, Ashton created a wholly unique wolf character in "Curse of the Werewolf." With his upright ears, piercing fangs and light gray appearance, Ashton's werewolf was unlike any before it on film. The next year, Ashton made Herbert Lom into a gruesome "Phantom of the Opera," a more viscerally acid-scarred version of the Phantom than the Lon Chaney or Jack Pierce versions.

In the late 1960s and early 1970s, Hammer slowed down their production slate, but Ashton still got the chance to create some memorable sequels, including work with David Prowse in "Frankenstein and the Monster from Hell." The impact of the Hammer films is not only the creation of new versions of the Monsters, but also the advent of color for a new generations of horror fans.

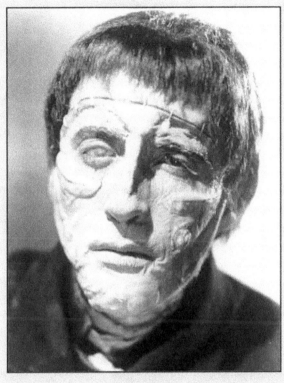

Christopher Lee in Phil Leakey's makeup as Frankenstein in "Curse of Frankenstein" (above). Below right, Ashton's unique wolf makeup for "Curse of the Werewolf." Below left, Lee is about to become mummified in Hammer's version of "The Mummy."

SCOTT ESSMAN

Dick Smith: Master of Illusions

In the postwar era, two preeminent makeup artists would surface at the fledgling NBC TV network: Dick Smith in New York and John Chambers in Los Angeles. In 1945, Dick Smith brought his perfected experiments with various makeup formulas to dozens of TV specials, soon serving as the New York-based station's first department head of makeup. In the late 1960s, moving from TV to film, Smith created his unforgettable old-age makeups for "Little Big Man," "The Godfather" and "The Exorcist," developing the makeup technique of creating overlapping facial appliances for his actors, now a standard in the industry. He also created an old vampire makeup character called Barnabus Collins with actor Jonathan Frid in the TV show and film, "Dark Shadows," a groundbreaker for both age and horror makeup.

Notably, "The Exorcist" also featured the first use of what Smith came to call "special makeup effects," where an actor's face or body changed on camera without the addition of optical effects. Linda Blair's rotating head, bulging neck and demonic configurations were all products of Smith's groundbreaking merger of makeup and special effects, and "The Exorcist" spawned a horde of makeup-oriented horror films, artists and fan organizations. Blair's appearance in the film became an icon, and in the 1970s waves of fans began writing letters of appreciation to Dick Smith wanting to get into the makeup effects business.

Dick Smith created unforgettable makeups by creating overlapping facial appliances, such as Jonathan Frid's makeup from "Dark Shadows" (above) and Linda Blair's makeup from "The Exorcist" (below).

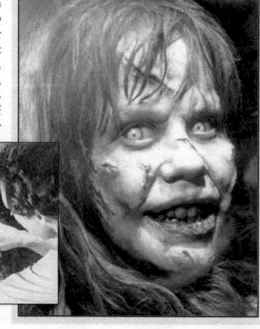

As a result, not only did Smith set standards with his makeup résumé, he also served as a mentor to a procession of young newcomers who would eventually make their own marks in the field. While residing on the East Coast, Smith kept up longstanding correspondence with two Los Angeles-based teenaged fans of his work, often shown in a select few publications, Famous Monsters of Filmland among them. Craig Reardon, whose credits went on to include "E.T.," "Poltergeist," and "Dreamscape," first connected with Smith in 1967, followed soon by Rick Baker. "I think that Dick was always waiting to share his enthusiasm for makeup and the things that he had learned about it into the ears of a receptive person," Reardon reflected. Noting Dick's contributions to his career, Baker concurred. "It was Dick's work more than anybody that inspired me to get into makeup," he said. "He set the standards that we all strive for, and his openness with formulas and techniques has really made makeup what it is today."

Dick Smith continued his active makeup work into the 1980s with films such as "Altered States" and "Amadeus" before retiring from on-set makeup application in 1987. However, he still works from his East Coast base, serving as a mentor to many new makeup artists through his professional makeup course. His legacy is equally strong as an innovator and spiritual father for the makeup effects industry.

SCOTT ESSMAN

John Chambers: Prosthetics Master

With very few and special exceptions, there is no more influential an individual in the modern world of special makeup effects than John Chambers. From his work in television's crucial first decades through groundbreaking cinematic triumphs as pivotal as "Planet of the Apes," Chambers 30-year career in Hollywood solidified his legacy as undeniable technical master and pioneer of both tutorial and ethical standards that have yet to be surpassed. Though he has been retired for more than a decade, Chambers left a legacy of excellence that continues to ripple through the work of his many peers and proteges.

In Los Angeles, starting in 1953, John Chambers brought his knowledge of medical prosthetics, first implemented for WWII veterans, to countless TV programs before moving onto feature films. Chambers did a variety of jobs, including the design of Spock's ears for "Star Trek" before undertaking a job that would garner him an honorary Oscar for makeup.

"Planet of the Apes," the first widely recognized film to successfully display prosthetically-produced characters on a large scale. Chambers' makeup design concept was for "Apes" was unprecedented and forever changed movie history. For the principal actors, chimps and orangutans were "T"-shaped, three-piece, appliance makeups which included a brow piece, upper lip, and lower lip; gorillas were a two-piece makeup. The principals' appliances were removed at the end of a day's shooting with an alcohol acetone solution that cut the glue and washed out the rubber without damaging it.

Chambers' experimentation led to a foam rubber that allowed the actors' skin to breathe comfortably. Forced to pioneer many production techniques to meet the demands of such a large-scale makeup show, Chambers claims, "we innovated everything." The most influential of his landmark practices was the advent of pre-painting the ape appliances.

John Chambers' large scale use of prosthetics in "Planet of the Apes" (such as on actor Roddy McDowell, above) earned him an honarary Oscar. At right, one of Chamber's "humanimals" from "Island of Dr. Moreau."

The proportions of the film, by any standard, were enormous: there were often as many as sixty make-up artists and more than forty hairdressers working every day; most of these craftspeople handed out masks, made sure that they fit, then colored around the actors' eyes so that their flesh was not exposed. On select shooting days, there were 160 extras with background masks on.

In 1976, Chambers undertook a film version of "Island of Dr. Moreau," starring Michael York. For the project, he created a variety of animal-human hybrids, including a BoarMan, BullMan, LionMan, BearMan, and the Sayer of the Law. A film adaptation of H.G. Wells classic story (which was remade again in 1996 with makeups by Stan Winston Studio), "Moreau's' Humanimals" featured Chambers' detailed approach for the planned makeups which significantly differed from the relatively simple hair appliances of the man-beast mutants in the 1933 version of the story, *Island of Lost Souls*. In contrast, "Moreau" was similar to Chambers' *Apes* projects in the intense amount and scope of the many required makeups — each of which took about four hours — filmed over seven weeks of shooting in the Caribbean.

Like Dick Smith, Chambers retired in the 1980s but has served as a mentor to young artists who left their stamps in makeup effects. Under Chambers' tutelage in the mid-1960s were Ken Chase, who would go on to create seamless age makeups in "Back to the Future," Tom Burman, who created myriad makeup effects in "Cat People," and Michael Westmore, the head of makeup for "Star Trek's" film-TV universe since 1987. Chambers passed away on August 25, 2001.

SCOTT ESSMAN

Rick Baker: Monster Maker

Rick Baker (right, with gorilla) applies vicious teeth to one of his gorilla warriors from Tim Burton's "Planet of the Apes." Below, Baker's Academy-Award winning make-up from "London."

Throughout the 100-year history of modern cinema, there are defining moments, onscreen events that divide time into a before and after, and forever change the way in which audiences perceive movies. Here is one such moment: actor David Naughton, writhing in pain in a bright London flat, screams in horror as he witnesses his hand slowly elongating in front of his eyes. Before we can fully digest this spectacle, he is hurled to the floor in convulsions only to have his spine, legs, and then, amazingly, his nose and jaw perform the same wrenching extension. With the aid of Rick Baker's revolutionary artistry and techniques, Naughton completes his transformation into a lycanthrope for "An American Werewolf in London," and so the face of movies was changed from that point forward.

Rick Baker has had a profound influence on movies of the past 20 years — he won the first official Academy Award for makeup on "American Werewolf." But he had made his mark long before that. While he was still a teenager, Baker observed his mentor Dick Smith create the groundbreaking age makeup on Dustin Hoffman in "Little Big Man" and a few years later worked on the rotating dummy head in "The Exorcist." In the mid-1970s, Baker got many of his own monster makeup assignments, including the demonic baby in "It's Alive!" and 'King Kong" for which Baker created and acted in a hand-made gorilla suit, one of his many ape characters for movies. Then, Baker was contacted by George Lucas to populate the famous Cantina scene with creatures.

Following "American Werewolf," Baker enjoyed many movie successes in the 1980s, including the realization of many realistic apes for "Greystoke" and "Gorillas in the Mist," and designing and producing a realistic radio-controlled giant for "Harry and the Hendersons." Baker also made a demon out of Michael Jackson and his dancers for the pioneering music video, "Thriller." At the end of the decade, he created convincing character makeups with Eddie Murphy in "Coming to America" and created dozens of imaginative creatures for the wild sequel, "Gremlins 2: The New Batch."

Into the 1990s, as hundreds of talented new people set up shops as makeup effects artists, only an elite few emerged successful enough to supervise their own movies. With CGI, or computer-generated imagery, gaining increased attention and threatening to replace special makeup effects, the role of makeup again faced reinvention and demanded a new type of artist comfortable with both methods. Nonetheless, the ongoing advances in makeup materials and application techniques has kept makeup relevant, as evidenced by Rick Baker's realistic character makeups in "Ed Wood," the Eddie Murphy vehicle "The Nutty Professor," and "Men in Black." Including last year's numerous makeups in "How the Grinch Stole Christmas," Baker now has six Academy Awards with the 2001 remake of "Planet of the Apes" likely leading to yet another Oscar nomination.

SCOTT ESSMAN

Stan Winston: Larger Than Life

While Rick Baker and his protégés were raising the stakes of makeup effects in the 1980s, another special makeup effects team gained equal status and respect for their efforts. Stan Winston had apprenticed at Disney Studios under long-running makeup department head Bob Schiffer and broke through with such prosthetic projects as "The Autobiography of Jane Pittman," which he co-created with Baker. Soon afterwards, Winston received one of the biggest prosthetics jobs of the period when his studio created the innovative makeups for "The Wiz." However, it was a modestly-budgeted sci-fi action film co-written and directed by James Cameron, a virtual nonentity at the time, that put Stan Winston on the makeup map.

"The Terminator" featured a range of special makeup effects, from metallic makeups and puppet heads of Arnold Schwarzenegger to humanoid makeup gags to full mechanical puppets. Winston and his team stretched the boundaries of what makeup effects could accomplish, continuing the trend with their giant alien queen in Cameron's "Aliens," the title characters for "Predator" and "Edward Scissorhands," and creating innovative makeup and effects for "Interview with the Vampire," with the on-set makeup skills of Michele Burke. In the early 1990s, there was "Terminator 2: Judgement Day," for which Winston created a variety of robotic effects and puppets.

Winston steadily diversified his shop so that Stan Winston Studio could handle any project in Hollywood, from makeups, to mechanical effects to full-scale creatures. His San Fernando Valley shop even has a complete machining department. Winston's loyal team of designers, sculptors, and mechanical people often stay with the studio from project to project.

Among Stan Winston's contributions to movie history are his creations from Terminator 2 (above), Jurassic Park (below), and Predator (inset).

Of all the material to come out of Winston's shop, the biggest project, in terms of sheer size and exposure was inarguably "Jurassic Park," for which full-size dinosaurs were manufactured and operated on set. Among the most memorable were the velociraptors and the Tyrannosaurus Rex. Winston repeated his skills with both "Jurassic Park" sequels, each time going further with dinosaur realism and movement.

From the "Terminator" years through the 1990s, many top-notch effects artists have remained at Stan Winston Studios, with notable exception being a pair of supervisors who left to form their own shop, Alec Gillis and Tom Woodruff, Jr. Amalgamated Dynamics, Inc. has featured Gillis and Woodruff's full-size mechanical abilities in projects ranging from "Tremors" and "Death Becomes Her" to "Starship Troopers."

Into the 21st century, Stan Winston has expanded his monstrous empire to include toy design, new media and directing films. His first such effort, "Pumpkinhead" was a cult horror favorite, and Winston plans to continue his directing efforts. His most notable new project was Steven Spielberg's "A.I. Artificial Intelligence," which found Winston and his extensive team constructing a team of futuristic robots. Over the same period of time in the year 2000, Stan Winston Studio was creating the robots and operating them on set while a separate team at the studio built the Spinosaurus and tyranodons for this year's "Jurassic Park III."

SCOTT ESSMAN

Ve Neill: The Many Faces of Fantasy

Makeup artist Ve Neill has been doing landmark makeup for films for over 20 years. Responsible for many of the most famous characters in Tim Burton's movies, Neill has won three Academy Awards - for Burton's "Beetlejuice" and "Ed Wood" plus another for "Mrs. Doubtfire" — while winning several other nominations. It goes without saying that Neill is a unique commodity in Hollywood in that she equally commands the art of applying both specialized prosthetic makeups and unique character and beauty makeups, and effortlessly travels between the two worlds. She began in the 1970s and has worked steadily since.

In 1987, for "The Lost Boys," the director, Joel Schumacher, wanted the vampires to look sexy, scary and ethereal. Ve did a test makeup on the actors, going for a very subtle look. "When you remove somebody's eyebrows they get the most bizarre look," Neill said.

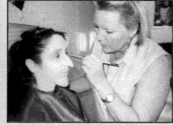

Ve Neill (bottom right) is responsible for some of the modern cinema's most recognizable makeups and characters.

"They became really otherworldly. Also we changed where the teeth would be: we did double fangs and did them on the incisors and the tooth right in front of it; they were spooky but kind of sexy in a real weird way." Greg's Cannom's original design for the vampires on The Lost Boys has been used on just about every vampire movie and TV show since then.

Soon, she got an interview with Tim Burton for "Beetlejuice." "Tim pretty much designs all of his characters and then you take his drawings and you go from there," she said. "When we first started testing Michael Keaton's makeup, I created a look just like one in the drawing that Tim had shown me, but he was so creepy, he was too real. He didn't want him to be that unsettling — he wanted him to be funny." Michael Keaton only worked a little over two weeks on the film, but his character became the life of the film, no irony intended.

When she was called by John Caglione and Doug Drexler to do the Big Boy Caprice makeup in "Dick Tracy," it was a unique process that led to a design for actor Al Pacino. "For three days Al and I sat around and tried on different noses and chins until we found a look that we liked, and one that Al was comfortable with," she said. Then, it was back to Tim Burton's world for "Edward Scissorhands." For that project, Ve said, "I think Johnny Depp really had a great deal to do with bringing that character to life. He really brought some heart and soul to it. Ultimately, Tim Burton designed the character, so Stan Winston and I just brought it to life. Stan had designed the makeup and we basically used the forehead piece that was designed and then he had sheets of different types of scars. Edward was supposed to innocent, so I gave him a look almost like a clown makeup."

Ve Neill went on to many successful projects in the 1990s, including the "Batman" sequels; she created Danny DeVito's makeup for The Penguin. "Again Tim Burton designed everything and Stan Winston sculpted the pieces and then I did all the test makeups and did all the actual application of the makeup, and I designed the colors used. She also became known for striking character makeups in all of her films recently including "A.I. Artificial Intelligence." "That is what I am good at — doing the application, being on the set, and making the department run smoothly," Neill noted. "I test my makeups before every movie I do, and I never stop learning. The part that I think is great about my career is the fact that I can do everything from beauty makeup to creatures and monsters. I think I have a nice broad spectrum of the craft, and if you want to be a well-rounded makeup artist that is what you have to do. I just feel so ecstatic about the fact that being a makeup artist is something that I have wanted to do ever since I was a child."

SCOTT ESSMAN

Makeup Today, Tomorrow, Always

GREG CANNOM

As a young man, Greg Cannom was fascinated by makeup in the movies, especially John Chambers' Sixth Finger makeup for "The Outer Limits" and Dick Smith's old vampire in "House of Dark Shadows." However, it wasn't until Smith's work in "The Exorcist" caught Cannom's eye that the budding artist decided to pursue make-up professionally. Three years after that film, Cannom contacted Rick Baker, who by 1976 was a leading makeup artist and creature creator in Hollywood. Their friendship led to Cannom joining Baker's team, at one time called "Baker's Dozen" on several films.

When Baker left "The Howling" to work on "American Werewolf in London," Cannom stayed behind working with colleague Rob Bottin and contributing to Robert Picardo's werewolf makeups. He helped with the gorilla effects in Baker's "The Incredible Shrinking Woman" and joined Baker in England for the filming of "Greystoke." Shortly thereafter, Cannom branched out on his own, getting the job of creating alien makeups for the sci-fi fantasy, "Cocoon."

Cannom created the grisly makeup effects for "Nightmare on Elm Street 3" then got the task of creating vampire makeups for "The Lost Boys." It was the look of the vampires that Cannom created on "Lost Boys" which has seemingly influenced many of the vampire films and TV shows that have come since. With his own shop, Greg Cannom Creations, Cannom stayed active in the late 1980s and early 1990s, working on many sci-fi, fantasy, and horror films, designing and executing the makeup effects.

Then Cannom got a dream job - creating creatures and makeups for Francis Ford Coppola's lavish take on "Bram Stoker's Dracula." Cannom created the memorable age makeup on Gary Oldman, then changed the actor into the striking wolf creature and bat creature, each an elaborate prosthetic design. For his efforts, Cannom won an Oscar for best makeup of 1992.

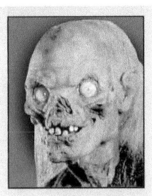

Above: Yagher's Crypt Keeper. Below, Cannom's makeup for Gary Oldman in "Dracula."

Cannom's string of successes continued when in the two years that followed, he created the title characters in the film's "Mrs. Doubtfire," which won him another Academy Award, and "The Mask," changing Jim Carrey into the delightfully zany green monster. By the mid-1990s, Cannom had also earned a reputation as a master old-age makeup specialist. In films ranging from "Forever Young," in which he aged Mel Gibson some 50 years, to "Roommates" where he believably aged Peter Falk, to "Titanic" where he made 86-year old Gloria Stuart into a woman over 100, Cannom's age work is second to none.

Into the late 1990s, Cannom continued to get choice assignments for his various fortés, including vampires in "Blade," old age makeups in "Bicentennial Man," and demons and gory effects in films including "Hannibal" and "Monkeybone." It would seem that Greg Cannom is a makeup artist who can tackle any assignment.

KEVIN YAGHER

For over fifteen years Kevin Yagher has been a forerunner in providing high-end special makeup effects for the entertainment industry. Yagher started in professional makeup in the early 1980s, later assisting Greg Cannom on films such as "Cocoon." He started his own business in 1985, when the art of special makeup effects was still in its adolescent stage. Beginning with such characters as Freddy Krueger in "A Nightmare on Elm Street Part 2" and Chucky in the "Child's Play" films, Kevin established himself as one of the top makeup effects artists. In fact, for the various "Elm Street" sequels and special appearances, he applied Robert Englund's Freddy Krueger makeup over 200 times!

Shortly after his work on "Child's Play," Kevin was approached by the producers of HBO's "Tales From the Crypt" to design and build the show's host, the Crypt Keeper. Kevin also directed all of the show's wrap-arounds, and several promotional spots, one of which earned him an Emmy. Kevin Yagher productions has worked on a variety of assignments, by developing and creating life-like creatures, aliens and humans with meticulous detail. In "Volcano," his company created the lava bombs, and in Paul Verhoeven's science-fiction film, "Starship Troopers" he created many realistic bodies and human gore effects.

For the Tim Burton hit "Sleepy Hollow," Yagher was a screenwriter and producer while also creating the many memorable makeup effects. In John Woo's "Face/Off," Yagher provided numerous gruesome effects: the film includes an operation sequence in which the facial skins of John Travolta and Nicholas Cage are removed and then switched. Woo was so pleased with the face switching effects that he cancelled the scheduled computer effects touch-up work.

Yagher continues to work actively in makeup effects though his writing and directing talents take him in a more "above the line" direction. However, he has no plans to leave makeup completely. As one of his early influences, Dick Smith, recently said, "Kevin's very skilled at his craft. His work is always very good."

STEVE JOHNSON

Every artist has his or her own signature – in Steve Johnson's case, it's usually the wide-open gaping mouths of his characters. Check his credits and you'll see for yourself. Of course, this has a double meaning, as Johnson's work is also always jaw-dropping.

When Rick Baker came to Houston, Texas for a convention in the late 1970s, the teenaged Johnson was one of the eager admirers who approached Baker, enthusiastically telling him that he wanted to be a makeup artist. Sensing the young man's passion, Baker encouraged him, telling Johnson to look Baker up should he ever move to Los Angeles. Not a long while went by before Johnson did just that and began an informal apprenticeship with Baker and another young makeup artist, Rob Bottin. Johnson spent those first few years on both Baker and Bottin projects, including "The Fog," "Humanoids From the Deep" and "An American Werewolf in London," where Johnson assisted with the creation of several puppets and effects.

Several years later, Johnson was working in the historic "Ghost Shop" established to create ghouls large and small for the film "Ghostbusters." Several Johnson creations were quite memorable in the film, including "Slimer," who found room in his huge mouth for all types of food when he wasn't sliming Bill Murray.

Johnson created frightening creatures for several other projects in the mid-1980s, including "Fright Night," an underrated vampire film, and "Poltergeist II" before branching out with his own company, XFX. Among the earliest XFX projects was James Cameron's "The Abyss," for which Johnson created benevolent aliens that had to work underwater, changing colors while maintaining a translucent appearance.

In the early 1990s, Steve Johnson's company provided brilliant vampire effects for John Landis' horror romp, "Innocent Blood," playfully labelled "A French Vampire in America." Not long after that, Johnson supervised the construction of Syl, the leading alien visage in "Species," based on H.R. Giger's designs. Johnson also did many tests and designs for suits in Tim Burton's aborted new version of "Superman" and built an enormous oversize animatronic title character for the never-completed film of "The Incredible Hulk."

Above: Bottin's werewolf from "The Howling." Below, Johnson's Onionhead ghost, popularly known as "Slimer."

In the late 1990s, Johnson was tasked with several huge projects, including numerous undersea creatures for "Sphere," robotic effects for "Virus," and a horde of believable robotic suits for "Bicentennial Man." Additionally, he created makeup and effects for many rock videos and TV commercials, including the characters in the unique Duracell Battery campaign. By the turn of the century, Johnson had moved his company into an elaborate new facility, and one of their first big projects was the sequel to "Blade."

ROB BOTTIN

Rob Bottin was only 14 years old when he first became an active participant in movie magic. His mentor, future Oscar-winner Rick Baker, may have been the best teacher a student of special makeup effects could ever hope to have. As Baker's special makeup apprentice, Bottin's first film assignment was Dino De Laurentiis' lavish 1976 remake of "King Kong". Their next job was working on the colorful aliens in the celebrated cantina sequence in George Lucas' "Star Wars" (1977). The neophyte effects technician soon started Rob Bottin Productions, his own effects company, at age 18. He received his first feature credit as special makeup effects designer and special effects designer on Joe Dante's "Piranha" (1978), and later did the monster effects on another Roger Corman feature,

"Humanoids From the Deep" (1980).

His career really took off with his special makeup effects (and a bit part as the decaying captain of a lost ship) in John Carpenter's "The Fog" (1980), and Joe Dante's "The Howling" (1981). For the latter, he created a special makeup milestone with his werewolf transformation. The werewolves in "The Howling" became animals without camera cuts or dissolves; Bottin's wolves' noses elongated and sprouted ears and hair. Much like mentor Rick Baker's work in "American Werewolf in London," and Dick Smith's effects in "Altered States," Bottin's wondrous creations in "The Howling" ushered in the era of special makeup effects.

Topping himself, Bottin reteamed with writer-director Carpenter for his 1982 remake of "The Thing". His outlandish, over-the-top special makeup effects may be viewed as Bottin's signature work. Myriad effects, including a husky dog that comes apart and transforms into a hideous monster, and a man whose head falls off of a human body and becomes a spider, were breathtaking. Bottin worked again with Dante, creating cartoonish creatures for the "It's A Good Life" segment of "Twilight Zone - The Movie" (1983) and the comic fantasy "Explorers" (1985).

In the mid-1980s, Bottin also created multiple characters for Ridley Scott's fantasy "Legend" and the robotic suit and makeup effects for Paul Verhoeven's "Robocop." It was his elaborate work on Verhoeven's sci-fi adventure "Total Recall" (1990) that finally won Bottin an Oscar. In the 1990s, Bottin's films included "Seven" and "Mission: Impossible" and he created numerous character makeups for "Fight Club." Always eager to direct feature films, Bottin has long been rumored to direct and create makeup for "Jason vs. Freddy," an all-out battle of horror heroes.

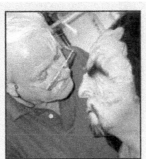

Above: Westmore designed the Klingon Martok, here applied by Dave Quashnick. Below: Westmore's "Raging Bull" make-up for Robert De Niro

MICHAEL WESTMORE

Living up to the legacy of your family name is hard enough – imagine having to do so when your father and five of your uncles were renowned makeup artists? This was the challenge that faced Michael Westmore, but even as a young man, Michael met the tasks ahead of him with great spirit and skills to match. The youngest of three brothers, all of whom did makeup, Michael began in the early 1960s as an apprentice to John Chambers. The two worked at Universal Studios, primarily on television projects such as "The Munsters," for which Michael was responsible of creating the look for Butch Patrick, aka Eddie Munster. After his apprenticeship, Michael continued working in TV, eventually getting his own series in 1974 with "Land of the Lost."

In the mid-1970s, Michael fortuitously began a seven-year continuous professional relationship with Sylvester Stallone. The first big project on which he and Michael worked? None other than "Rocky" for which Westmore created the bloody fight makeups for both Stallone and Carl Weathers, often at the same time! Since there was no money in the small film's budget to hire another makeup artist, Westmore would apply one makeup, let it dry, and attend to the other actor in the meantime. Of course, the film went on to make history, winning an Oscar for best picture, and both Stallone and Westmore's careers were forever cemented.

In 1980, Michael got a job that was originally offered to Dick Smith, "Raging Bull." More realistic and gritty a boxing film than "Rocky," Raging Bull provided Michael with the chance to create horrifying makeup effects for star Robert DeNiro, who gets badly battered in one fight sequence. Westmore meticulously designed facial appliances for DeNiro which would allow for blood to squirt through hidden tubes with the help of a syringe device.

In 1987, he was offered a job that would continue through the rest of his career – supervising makeup for the "Star Trek" universe, including films, TV shows, and special events and exhibits. First up was "Star Trek: The Next Generation," for which he worked with Gene Roddenberry to determine the looks and colors of the makeups, including the Data character and the Klingons. In the "Voyager" and "Deep Space Nine" series and films since "Star Trek: Generations," Westmore has been in charge of all makeups and alien characters, winning numerous awards in the process. He has been nominated for more Emmy Awards for his TV work than any other makeup artist in history. In 2000, Westmore signed on to supervise one more "Star Trek" series with the planned fall 2001 debut of "Star Trek: Enterprise."

Drawing on his 40+-year career and considerable knowledge of makeup application and laboratory work, Westmore is one of the most respected makeup artists working in the business today.

SCOTT ESSMAN

MICHELE BURKE

"Every time you work in makeup, you are met with new challenges," said two-time Academy Award-winning makeup artist Michele Burke. "You have to be on your toes so you can do the budget, design and apply makeup, and work within a large creative mass of people." With credits as diverse as "Bram Stoker's Dracula," "Interview with the Vampire," and "Austin Powers II: The Spy Who Shagged Me," Michele Burke is a self-described "makeup artist who designs and creates characters and unusual beings" in an industry where women who do so are a rare commodity.

Having originally immigrated to Canada from Ireland, she began doing fashion and beauty makeup, but she felt like her real calling was in the movies. "To be a true makeup artist, I felt that you had to do everything," she remembered, "so I decided to branch out beyond fashion, even though I still do a major amount of beauty work today. I think I have such a good foundation in the prosthetic world because I know how to do really subtle work with fine detailing and a soft touch."

Burke's first big break came when she was called to work on the 1981 French-Canadian production, "Quest for Fire:" the experience garnered Burke an Academy Award for best makeup. She followed her success on "Quest for Fire" with two other films dealing with primitive man - "Iceman" and "Clan of the Cave Bear" - in both cases, working with future Star Trek makeup supervisor Michael Westmore.

In the early 1990s, Burke received the assignment of designing the makeup and hair for all of the characters in "Bram Stoker's Dracula," while makeup artist Greg Cannom created the old age look, the Bat creature and Wolf creature for Gary Oldman. "Initially, I wasn't involved in the hair part at all," Burke recollected, "but when I came aboard, the director, Francis Ford Coppola, said that he wanted one person to spearhead the look of the makeup and hair, and what each character should look like. He wanted me to make drawings of each character and all the looks that they would have on the show, including Dracula's old-age hairstyle."

Burke's achievements on Bram Stoker's Dracula garnered her another Academy Award for best makeup, leading to her next major project, "Interview With the Vampire." Burke's ideology was based on her experiences working on large-scale films. "When you have shows with special makeup, the faster you are, the better!" she said. "I think that is one of my fortés, being able to work it out so that we as a makeup team can pump out these actors to the director, and we're not spending time during production touching them up." With the combination of Burke's versatility and the prosthetic innovations from Stan Winston's team, "Interview With The Vampire" contains an array of striking makeups, from Tom Cruise's various likenesses to the startling vein effects on the other vampire characters.

Following "Vampire," Burke was makeup supervisor on many late 1990s films, leading to her work on the "Austin Powers" sequel, where she led a team which created Doctor Evil, Mini-Me and the Austin Powers character. By fall of 1999, Michele Burke started yet another show as makeup department head for the big-budget thriller, "The Cell," starring Jennifer Lopez. In the spring of 2001, she began department heading Steven Spielberg's "Minority Report." Though she has seemingly conquered all her makeup goals, Burke has one left. "In the future, I would like to manufacture some of my own products," she revealed, "but I don't think I will ever stop doing makeup because I see it as a form of art and creativity through which I constantly have a need to express myself. And that fascination with people and characters will never end."

Above, Burke's makeup for Tom Cruise in "Vampire;" Below, Tippett works on an Imperial Walker in "Empire."

PHIL TIPPETT

When George Lucas asked Rick Baker to create additional creatures for the famed cantina sequence in "Star Wars," few realized that the collection of artists that Baker recruited would become a "who's who" of modern special effects masters. In addition to Baker himself, the young team included Jon Berg, Doug Beswick, Rob Bottin, Laine Liska, and Phil Tippett. This tightly-knit group, many of whom were stop-motion animators, went on to revolutionize the course of special creature effects in many of the landmark effects-oriented films of the past 20 years, Tippett among the most prominent.

A sizable portion of "Star Wars"' special effects crew had worked together at fledgling production houses in Southern California during the late 1960s and early 1970s. Berg and Tippett had paid their dues at Cascade Pictures where they worked on TV commercials creating stop-motion animation. The wild success of "Star Wars" - which included a Tippett-animated chess game - simultaneously created both a new demand for effects and an industry to support it.

Lucas immediately began production on "The Empire Strikes Back, which included one of the most stirring stop-motion sequences of the era: the Imperial Walker battle on the ice planet, Hoth. Tippett, Berg and Beswick, all ILM fixtures, created the animation. In 1981, a breakthrough arrived when Stuart Ziff, working with Tippett at ILM, created the Go-Motion FigureMover, a device that allowed Tippett's animation to move more fluidly in "Dragonslayer."

Tippett, still at ILM, created stop-motion creatures for Lucas' "Ewok" TV movies and shot a stop-motion dinosaur film entitled "Prehistoric Beast" in his home garage. This project would forecast a new wave of creature animation for the industry a decade later. Having formed Tippett Studio in the wake of independent assignments, Tippett developed the stop-motion ED-209 for Paul Verhoeven's "Robocop" and the multi-faceted "Robocop 2" for the sequel, again collaborating with "Star Wars" cantina designer Rob Bottin.

Based on his lasting interest in animating dinosaurs, Tippett created test stop-motion footage for "Jurassic Park," detailed treatments of the kitchen sequence with the velociraptors and the attack sequence with the Tyrannosaurus Rex. His work was comprised of stop-motion reference puppetry mixed with storyboards and resembled the animation in "Prehistoric Beast." After Steven Spielberg saw the footage, he inked Tippett to create stop-motion dinosaur animations to match Stan Winston's live-action mechanical beasts. Then ILM developed CGI dinosaur tests (originally meant for only a few shots) that were so convincing, it was obvious that they would eliminate the need for any stop-motion work.

Tippett felt as if he was becoming "extinct," but Spielberg was attached enough to Tippett's work to retain him as "dinosaur supervisor." In fact, ILM's computer animators, identically utilized Tippett's original animation in the two stop-motion test sequences.

The success of CGI in "Jurassic Park" was certainly not lost on Phil Tippett himself. Not one to become "extinct," Tippett acquired an additional building for his Berkeley complex, housing over 100 workstations for the 80+ computer animators he hired to create many species of giant bugs for "Starship Troopers." Where "Jurassic Park" featured some 50 CGI shots, "Troopers" required nearly 200 CGI shots. Though his shop has been actively creating CGI animation ever since, Tippett predicts he will someday complete his stop-motion swan song when the time and situation are appropriate.

TOM BURMAN

Starting in the 1960s, Tom Burman has been at the forefront of makeup artistry. In 1966, he was working at 20th Century Fox Studios when he overheard producers wanting to get the person responsible for the makeup in "The List of Adrian Messenger" to do a new movie at the studio called "Planet of the Apes." Burman told them that the main artist behind "Messenger" was John Chambers, and the two paired up in January 1967 to work on the landmark project. With Chambers and Burman doing everything from the initial sculptural concepts to the meticulous laboratory work, nearly nine months was spent on the project. When the film debuted in the spring of 1968, the makeups received universal praise, earning Chambers a special honorary Oscar.

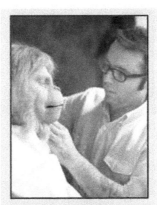

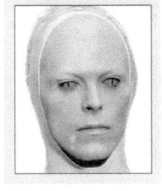

Above: Burman's makeup for "Planet of the Apes;" Below: David Bowie's in "Man Who Fell to Earth."

Burman and Chambers worked closely together through the mid-1970s, co-creating projects including "Island of Dr. Moreau" in which they created numerous Humanimals. Of course, the time came for Burman to create projects on his own, and several of them were wholly unique in their conception and execution. In 1976, he created David Bowie's alien character in "The Man Who Fell to Earth," and in 1977, Burman provided Steven Spielberg with a group of small aliens characters for the climactic ending of "Close Encounters of the Third Kind." The next year, Burman got the task of creating pod people and makeup effects for an update of the classic sci-fi horror film "Invasion of the Body Snatchers."

In the 1980s, Burman continued his string of makeup successes. He created numerous demonic effects for 1981's "The Beast Within" and the amazing transformations and effects for the following year's "Cat People," one of the early-1980s landmark films for special makeup. Among the many special surprises in the film is a scene where Natassia Kinski transforms into a black panther!

With his wife, Bari Drieband-Burman, Tom's Burman Studio has been responsible for some of the best makeup and effects work of the 1980s and 1990s. The Burman Studio also created the extensive transformation makeups for the second remake, "Body Snatchers." Tom and Bari continue to work actively, as well as Tom's two sons, Robert and Barney, who are both talented makeup artists in their own rights.

SCOTT ESSMAN

TODD TUCKER

As the creative force behind Wonderworld Entertainment, and as one of the key special effects makeup artists and creature creators at Greg Cannom's studio, Todd Tucker creates prosthetic makeups, creature suits, and puppets that are used for both film and television. "Originally, I was going to be a cartoonist," Tucker said. "All through high school I worked on my illustration portfolio. I was always interested in horror and fantasy movies, so in 1985, I looked into schools that taught special effects makeup. Luckily, I met up with a couple of excellent special effects artists, Matt Rose and Steve Wang. They showed me sculpting and painting techniques and taught me what I needed to know." For the next five years, Tucker practiced in his garage, building his portfolio before moving to Los Angeles to try his hand at the movie business.

He followed the nascent Rose and Wang who collaborated on the creature for Predator among many others coming to Hollywood from San Jose. "I showed Greg Cannom my portfolio and he liked my work," Tucker stated, "so he hired me that day and I started the following week." Tucker found himself working as a sculptor, painter, moldmaker and fabricator over the next five years on projects including Bram Stoker's Dracula, Mrs. Doubtfire, and The Mask. "Cannom hires people who are multi-talented: people who can sculpt, paint, mold, fabricate," observed Tucker. "They need to know everything. I jumped around quite a bit, which is fortunate because often times, people who work in a shop can get pigeonholed into one department like moldmaking, seaming, or running foam. I was able to work in all different aspects of the shop then work on set with the puppets and the makeups."

Due to his versatility, most of Tucker's assignments became steadily more interesting and challenging. "As the years went on, I became more involved in sculpting and designing the characters," he recalled, "and within four years, I became one of the shop supervisors and was heading up my own shows through Cannom Creations, including Jingle All the Way, Steel, A Simple Wish, and Kull the Conqueror." During this time, though he was successful, Tucker never lost sight of his boyhood dream. "I always knew that my final goal was to write and create my own stories," he said. "That was my wish since I was a little kid to follow in the footsteps of Steven Spielberg, George Lucas and Jim Henson and create worlds of characters."

Laboring at night and on weekends while he worked for Cannom Creations, Tucker formed Wonderworld Entertainment, then wrote scripts, created original character makeups and creature suits, and filmed three-minute "teasers" for two of his projects: the first one, Wolvy, is the tale of a wacky werewolf character, his buddy, Gus, a four-armed abominable snow monster, his nemesis, Willy Weasel, and Willys pair of crusher bodyguards, called the Thug Brothers. For Wolvy, Tucker designed and built all of the character elements, produced and directed the action, and performed as the title character in a head-to-toe werewolf suit with a mechanical head. His second such endeavor, The Underworld, features a ghostly-white demon named Luth, his menacing sidekick, Scythe, and their plans to imprison the world above.

Above: Tucker's diverse work touches many facets of make-up and prosthetic design. Below: Walas' "Fly."

For young people, who, like himself a decade ago, want to break into makeup and creature design professionally, Tucker recommends a path with equal parts persistence and self-education. "The best thing to do is get as many books, instructional materials, and videos that you could get your hands on, and practice, practice, practice," he instructed. "Sculpt, paint, learn how to run foam, apply makeup, everything you can. Start building a portfolio of your best work. Once you feel confident that you have enough knowledge and talent, start presenting your work. Never think that you're at a point when you can't learn any more. Always remember, if you really want something, its up to you to make it happen."

CHRIS WALAS

When Chris Walas was painting Halloween masks at Don Post Studios in the mid-1970s, he probably had no idea of the wonders that awaited him. With a string of successes second only to Rick Baker and Rob Bottin, Walas was to become one of the kings of movie monsters in the 1980s. Though he has retired from his trade to work as a film director, Walas created a legacy that will stand for all time.

In the late 1970s, both Walas and Robert Short were recruited by "Star Wars" effects alumni Jon Berg and Phil Tippett who were looking for budding creature people to work on a low budget film, "Piranha." Although Short and Tippett liked their tenure at Don Post's, "Piranha" represented the chance to work on a feature film. With undersea creatures by the effects team and special makeup by a teenaged Rob Bottin, Joe Dante's "Piranha" was a cult hit and set Walas' career in motion.

He soon left to work at Industrial Light and Magic where Tippett and Berg had both gone, creating many effects for the creature department, such as the melting faces in the climactic opening of the Ark at the end of "Raiders of the Lost Ark." Separately from ILM, Walas also took his share of makeup and effects projects, such as creating the notorious exploding head in David Cronenberg's "Scanners."

In 1983, Joe Dante brought Walas back to his team to create the numerous and expressive creatures for "Gremlins." With a short pre-production period, Walas created prototypes for the cuddly Mogwai and evil Gremlins, then worked out of a "creature trailer" on the set, providing Dante's comic film with all types of puppeted characters good and bad. The project was enormous by any standards, and Walas worked furiously, even breaking his foot while stepping out of the trailer on a particularly hectic day in the shoot!

Another Walas' project was no less ambitious than either of his two previous projects. Cronenberg's "The Fly" involved the deterioration of Jeff Goldblum's Seth Brundle character into a 6'4" fly-man. Conceived as an internal illness rather than a quick transformation, the film provided Walas with numerous stages of makeup. Several additional effects rounded out the project, which garnered Walas an Academy Award for makeup.

Needless to say, Chris Walas celluloid resume has provided films with some of the most imaginative rubber monsters in cinema history.

ABOUT THE AUTHOR

Scott Essman has been writing about makeup and movie craftsmanship since 1995. As part of his company, **Visionary Cinema**, Essman has also created memorable tributes to makeup history, including special events to honor Dick Smith, John Chambers, and Jack Pierce. In 1998, his tribute to the makeup for "The Wizard of Oz" was celebrated on Hollywood Boulevard at the historic Mann's Chinese Theater. In 2000, Essman published his first book, "Freelance Writing for Hollywood," and that same year, he published a 48-page special magazine about the work of Universal Studios' makeup legend, Jack Pierce. In 2001, he is joining with Universal to nominate Pierce for a star on Hollywood Boulevard's Walk of Fame, and in 2003, he is planning to commemorate the 100th birthday of Hollywood — both the city and the movies.

A TRIBUTE TO JACK PIERCE: THE MAN BEHIND THE MONSTERS

Today's artists still view Pierce's work as a relevant force in the annals of cinema crafts. A group of top Hollywood craftspeople has gathered to pay tribute to the often-overlooked pioneer. In the show, JACK PIERCE—THE MAN BEHIND THE MONSTERS, dozens of makeup and costume personnel, actors, and technical experts united to honor the man with a live dramatic show in Pasadena, California.

"I believe that the greats of Hollywood should not be forgotten," said costume designer Jennifer McManus. "People today should study what they did in order to further themselves." Her husband, makeup supervisor Robert Burman, concurs. "I wanted to be involved in something that touches everybody's inner kid," said Burman, a third generation Hollywood craftsman. "Working on this tribute has also been an opportunity to discover things about our heritage. For instance, I learned that my own grandfather sculpted and made molds for most of Jack Pierce's prosthetics and props in the 1940s, including the actual silver-tipped cane from "The Wolf Man." These guys were the forefathers of all of the work that we're doing today."

With vignettes selected from throughout his life—hosted by an actor playing 79-year-old Pierce as the show's narrator—JACK PIERCE—THE MAN BEHIND THE MONSTERS illustrated his greatest work in a one-night-only multi-media play, featuring 15 very special "character" appearances on stage, from the Frankenstein Monster and his Bride, to the Wolf Man and The Man Who Laughs. Additionally, several historical characters from the time period were re-created. Pierce's genius as a makeup artist is indicative of a unique creative period of time in movie history. Pierce and the other craftspeople who brought this work to life at the dawn of the sound age should forever be remembered by contemporary moviemakers.

For more information about the event, write to scottessman@yahoo.com or visit the website at www.jackpierce.com.

A WHOLE NEW MUMMY

On July 22, 2008, Universal Studios Home Entertainment will unleash a brand new DVD of *The Mummy* (1932). As part of the new packaging, expect a documentary about Jack Pierce, makeup legend portrayed herein this book (and below, left). A team of makeup artists led by Rob Burman recreated several of Pierce's makeups for the occasion. Foremost among them were the Frankenstein Monster, the Mummy (Ardath Bey version) and the Wolf Man (below, right) with specific makeup for the Wolf Man created by Lufeng Qu. Expertly, the documentary was produced by Constantine Nasr of New Wave Entertainment. Additional content includes feature commentary by Rick Baker, Bob Burns, Steve Haberman, and Brent Armstrong.

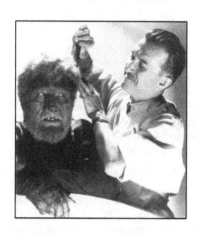

HUMANOIDS ON THE LOOSE

Look for a feature film remake of *Creation of the Humanoids*. Here are photos from a September 2007 green screen test shoot. The feature version will be shot in 2008 and released in 2009.

DIRECTED BY – THE CINEMA QUARTERLY
Current Issues for Sale

Issue #7 – **January 2008** - *$9.95* via Amazon.com as of February 2008

Davis Guggenheim – Frank Darabont – Jeffrey Blitz – Michael Katleman – James Wan – Robert Wise – THE MUMMY 75th ANNIVERSARY – THE SOPRANOS (3 directors plus Drea de Matteo and Lorraine Bracco) – WHERE WERE YOU IN 1982? - Richard Kelly – Brian Cook – Ben Affleck – Bobby Logan - BLADE RUNNER: THE FINAL CUT (64 Pages)

Issue #6 – **November 2006** - *$12.00 PostPaid*

Joe Dante – Richard Linklater – Ryan Murphy – Phillip Noyce – Guillermo Del Toro – Rob Bottin – Walter Hill – Mary Harron – James Gunn – Larry Clark – Peter Jackson – Michael Cuesta – Raw Feed - DRACULA / FRANKENSTEIN 75th ANNs – Nick Nolte – Samuel L. Jackson – Francisco Lorite - Tex Avery (56 Pages)

Issue #5 – **March 2006** - *$10.00 PostPaid*

Peter Jackson & King Kong DVD – The Sci Fi Boys – What is Your SCI-Q – Naomi Watts – Ray Harryhausen interview – DR. JEKYLL AND MR. HYDE ('32) – Editing King Kong '05 – Willis O'Brien Exclusive (36 Pages)

Issue #4 – **November 2005** - *$15.00 PostPaid*

Peter Jackson & Kings of Kong – Alejandro Jodorowsky – Terence Fisher – William Friedkin – Dario Argento – ACTION MOVIES – Renny Harlin – Paul Verhoeven – ACTORS ON DIRECTORS – Kate Montgomery – John Gray – John McNaughton – George Romero – Béla Lugosi Legacy – Willis O'Brien DVD – Alan Pakula book – Robert Wise appreciation (60 Pages)

SPECIAL ISSUE – **A CENTURY OF CREATURE PEOPLE** – History of Movie Makeup–$20.00 PostPaid, also on Amazon.com, TBA

Issue #3 – May 2004 – STAR WARS – SOLD OUT

Issue #2 – Winter 1999 – JOHN BOORMAN – SOLD OUT

Issue #1 – Fall 1998 – BRYAN SINGER – SOLD OUT

To Order Issues – Send Check/Money Order for **Total** with Order Details to Scott Essman at DIRECTED BY:

Scott Essman
DIRECTED BY
P.O. Box 1722
Glendora, CA 91740
visionarycinema@yahoo.com

Allow 3 Weeks for Checks to Clear and Shipping to Process / All Orders are Domestic 1st Class USPS

www.directed-by.com

WANT TO MAKE MONSTER MASKS LIKE A HOLLYWOOD PRO?

WANT AN INSIDE TRACK ON THE STEP-BY-STEP PROCESS?

WELL HERE ARE THE DVDS THAT YOU'VE BEEN WAITING FOR!

MONSTER MOVIE MASKS SERIES
A BRAND NEW DVD SET

Summit, New Jersey, April 1, 2007 – When you think of classic monster masks, you conjure the great Don Post masks of the 1960s and 1970s. Who could forget the iconic images of Dracula, Frankenstein's Monster, the Wolf Man, and the Mummy walking neighborhoods during Halloween? Masks are so ubiquitous in our society, even Hollywood monster stalwarts like Rick Baker have at one time made masks as a business. Well, ArtMolds, a New Jersey-based sculpture studio, is now presenting two 60-minute DVDs which explore the entire process from first conceiving your masks through preparing and finishing them. Presented and demonstrated by special effects artist Omar Sfreddo (SPIDER-MAN 2) and prop master Anthony Giordano (SATURDAY NIGHT LIVE), the two discs priced at $29.95 ($49.95 for both) are available for immediate purchase.

Discs are available exclusively at www.artmolds.com. 1-866-ARTMOLDS.

DETAIL – DISC ONE
Part One is packed with the comprehensive Molding & Casting Latex Masks process, including:

* Materials Required
* Finishing the Sculpt
* Preparing Clay Walls
* Creating the Plaster Mold
* Building Pry Points
* Demolding
* Pouring the Casting
* Demolding the Finished Mask

DETAIL – DISC ONE
Part Two follows up from One with the Finishing and Painting Latex Masks process, including:

* Materials Required
* Trimming the Mask
* Masking Repairs
* Using the Air Brush
* Shading and Highlighting
* Painting Veining
* Teeth and Eyes
* Final Finishes

© Copyright: 2007
Association of Lifecasters
International.
All Rights Reserved.

Price: $29.95 Each Disc
$49.95 Both Discs

TRT: 60 Minutes Each Disc
Rating: PG / Language: English

PUBLICITY CONTACT
Visionary Cinema
Scott Essman
(626) 963-0635

visionarycinema@yahoo.com

CPSIA information can be obtained
at www.ICGtesting.com
Printed in the USA
LVHW060106150921
697842LV00021BA/673